Introduction

This book contains 44 stencil designs of wild and cultivated American fruits and flowers. Here are delicate sprays of flax and lily of the valley, well-stocked baskets of tropical and temperate fruits and even a plate of papaya, pear and cantaloupe. Here you will also find designs suitable for use as corners and borders. Now, with the stencils in this book, you can transform your surroundings into bright and colorful orchards and meadows.

These stencils can be cut out and used again and again. Border elements can be repeated indefinitely to form frames and borders, and all designs can be flopped to reverse the image for symmetrical repetition. The illustrations on the covers give examples of attractive color patterns.

The designs can be used for decorating walls, floors, furniture, fabrics, tin, leather and almost any other surface. All materials needed are inexpensive and easy to find in most well-stocked hardware or art-supply stores. The method is easily mastered and projects quickly completed.

LIST OF MATERIALS

boiled linseed oil
turpentine
rags
stencil knife and blades
knife sharpener or carborundum stone
large knitting needles or ice pick
cutting surface (glass, wood, etc.)

masking tape
paint
textile paint (for fabric)
stenciling brushes
newspaper
fine sandpaper
desk blotters (for fabric)
varnish (for floors, wood, tin)
#4 artists' brush

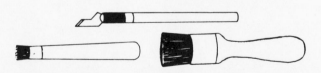

Stencil knife and two stenciling brushes of different sizes.

First, cut out an entire page (= stencil plate) from the book with a pair of scissors. When more than one design appears on a page, a dotted line serves as the cutting guideline for separating each design onto a distinct stencil plate. The margin of ¾ inch or more around the design makes the stencil sturdy and durable while in use and protects the surrounding areas from paint when stenciling.

The pages of this book are of medium-weight manila paper, which must be treated with oil to make it tough, leathery and impervious to moisture. Oiled manila will become semi-translucent, allowing light to penetrate slightly. A knife blade will cut through an oiled plate more easily. The oiling process takes place after the plate (page) is cut from the book but before the blacked-in areas of the design are cut out, so there will be no chance of bending or ripping delicate ties (bridge areas) when applying the oil.

A mixture of 50% *boiled* linseed oil and 50% turpentine is applied with a rag to both sides of the plate until it is thoroughly saturated. Using a thumbtack, the plate is then hung to dry. It will dry to the touch in about 10 minutes. Any excess can be wiped off with a dry rag or the plate can be allowed to dry for a longer period. The rag should then be immersed in water until it can be incinerated or removed by regular garbage disposal service. Spontaneous combustion can occur if the rag is stored for later use.

The stencil knife is used for cutting out the small pieces through which the paint will reach the surface to be decorated. Only the solid black areas of each design are cut out. Suitable cutting surfaces for this task are hard wood, a piece of plate glass with the edges taped, or a stack of old newspapers. The oiled stencil plate is placed on the cutting surface and allowed to move freely. Grasp the stencil knife as you would a pencil. Apply even pressure for the entire length of a curve or line. Frequent lifting of the knife causes jagged, uneven edges. The small details of the stencil design are cut out first and larger areas last to prevent weakening the plate before cutting is completed. Sharpen the blade frequently on a carborundum stone or knife sharpener.

Cutting requires careful and accurate work. A jagged line or ragged corner will stencil exactly that way in every impression of the stencil plate.

The narrow bridges of paper between the cut-out areas in the design are known as ties. If you accidentally cut through a tie, apply tape to both sides of the tear and replace the tape when needed. Circles and small dots are difficult to cut with a knife. Various large needles can be used to punch out the circles. Ice picks and different-size knitting needles work well. Carefully use the knife or a small piece of fine sandpaper to trim and smooth the edges.

Paints used for stenciling can be water-base or turpentine-base. Any paint used must be mixed to a fairly thick consistency. Acrylic paint is an excellent water-base paint because it is fast-drying and easy to clean up. Acrylics are sold in tubes or jars and come in the right consistency for stenciling. Japan paints come in small 8-ounce cans and must be thinned slightly with turpentine. Turpentine-base paints must be allowed to dry for 24 hours. Both acrylic and japan paint dry to a flat finish. As soon as stenciling is completed, brushes are cleaned, using water for water-base paints and turpentine for oil- or turpentine-base paints.

Stenciling on fabrics requires textile paints or inks made especially for decorating on fabric. Textile paints and inks come either water- or turpentine-soluble and are mixed thinner than regular paints. The fabric must be prewashed or drycleaned to remove any sizing and allow for shrinkage. Blotters must be used underneath the fabric to absorb excess moisture and paint. After the stenciled fabric has dried, ironing will set the textile paint or ink and make the colors permanent and washable. All these coloring mediums can be purchased at an art-supply store.

Brushes used for stenciling are cylindrical. The bristles are cut all the same length, forming a circular flat surface of bristle ends. Stencil brushes come in various sizes. A good selection of sizes would be ¼ inch in diameter, ½ inch in diameter, and 1 inch in diameter. A clean brush is used each time a new color is introduced.

Stenciling begins by securing the stencil plate on two sides with masking tape to the object being stenciled. If the plate is not secure, the action of the stencil brush will cause the design to smear. The brush is grasped like a pencil but held perpendicular to the work surface. Dip only the flat bottom of the bristles into the paint. Do not overload the brush with paint,

or it will run under the plate and ruin the design. Have several sheets of newspaper nearby for pouncing out the freshly loaded brush. Pouncing is a hammerlike movement that disperses the paint throughout the bristles. When an even speckling of paint is evident on the newspaper, the brush is ready for use. Stippling is the proper term for the rapid up-and-down motion of the brush over the stencil plate. Stippling continues until the openings in the plate are completely filled in with color.

Masking tape is used to keep different colors clean and separate if you desire to use more than one color for a single stencil plate. The varying parts of the design are masked with tape as each color is transferred. Changing the masking tape is done without removing the plate from the project being stenciled.

Designs that can be used to form borders and frames appear throughout the book. To form the border, repeat the design continuously, matching the edges, left to right or right to left.

As soon as stenciling with any plate is finished, the plate is wiped gently with a rag or sponge dampened with water or turpentine depending on the paint in use. This increases the life expectancy of the stencil plate by helping prevent the accumulation of paint around the edges of the design.

Colors can be lightened by the addition of white and grayed and neutralized by the addition of a small amount of the complementary color. Red and green are complements as are blue and orange, yellow and purple. The grayer the color the more faded and aged the final result. Metallic bronzing powders added to paint give the appearance of iridescence. Darker colors mixed to a thinner consistency with varnish or acrylic polymer over a light ground give the effect of translucency. Sanding the stenciled design with fine sandpaper will make it appear worn. Stencilwork on floors, woodwork and tin should be protected with several coats of a good varnish.

A more detailed and specific account of the art of stenciling is contained in *The Complete Book of Stencilcraft* (Dover, 0-486-25372-4), by JoAnne C. Day.

1 Cyclamen

2 Daffodils and Narcissi

3 Rose corner

4   Abutilon border

5   Tulips

7 Columbine

8   Flax

11   Dicentra (Bleeding Heart)

12 Flax and Campanula

13 Gaillardia and Coreopsis

15 Irises and Roses

16   Pineapple, Cantaloupe, Watermelon and Peaches in a basket

18 Peach basket

19 Peach basket

17 Cherry basket

22 Peonies

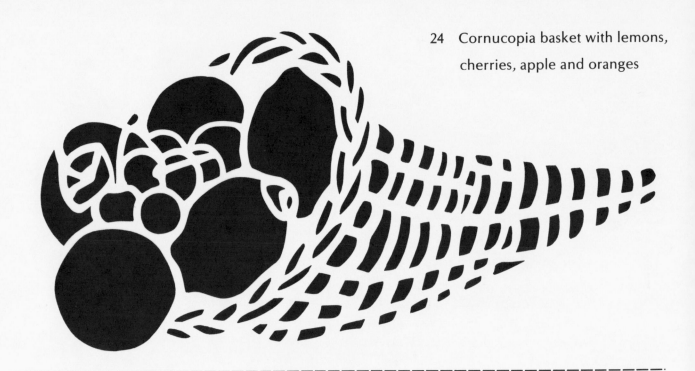

24 Cornucopia basket with lemons,
    cherries, apple and oranges

25 Rose basket

27 Papaya, Pear and Cantaloupe plate

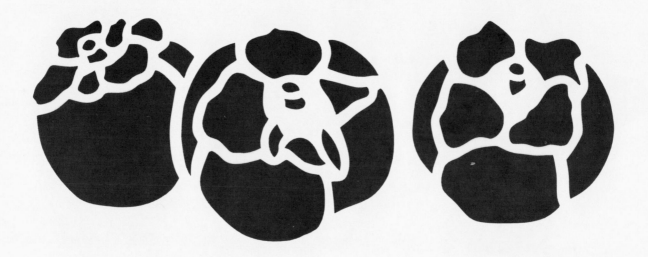

29 Grape, Apple and Pear basket

32   Campanula vertical border

31   Trillium vertical border

33   Trillium corners

34   Mixed flower basket

36   Buttercup corner

35   Buttercup corner

38 Peaches

43 Apple bushel basket

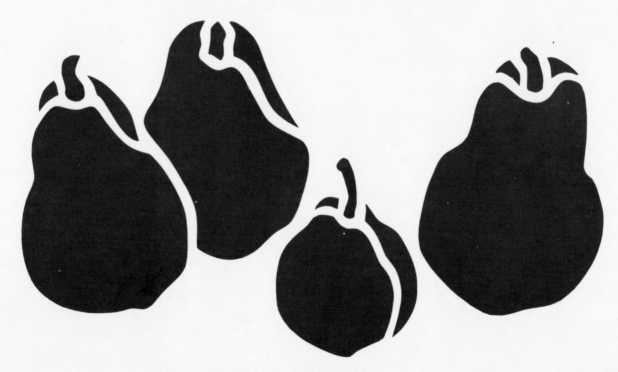

44 Pears